EDGE
BOOKS™

A FIELD GUIDE TO

Goblins, Gremlins, AND OTHER Wicked Creatures

BY A. J. SAUTTER

CAPSTONE PRESS
a capstone imprint

Edge Books are published by Capstone Press,
1710 Roe Crest Drive, North Mankato, Minnesota 56003
www.capstonepub.com

Library of Congress Cataloging-in-Publication Data
Sautter, Aaron.
A field guide to goblins, gremlins, and other wicked creatures / by A.J. Sautter.
pages cm.—(Edge books. Fantasy field guides)
Includes bibliographical references and index.
Summary: "Describes the features and characteristics of wicked and mischievous
fantasy creatures in a quick-reference format"—Provided by publisher.
ISBN 978-1-4914-0689-2 (library binding)
ISBN 978-1-4914-0693-9 (paperback)
ISBN 978-1-4914-0697-7 (eBook PDF)
1. Animals, Mythical—Juvenile literature. 2. Monsters—Juvenile literature. I. Title.
GR825.S277 2015
001.944—dc23   2014010193

Editorial Credits
Sarah Bennett, designer; Kazuko Collins, layout artist;
Kelly Garvin, media researcher; Katy LaVigne, production specialist

Photo Credits
Capstone Press: Colin Ashcroft, 1, 7, 13, Jason Juta, 22, 25, 26, Martin Bustamante,
cover, 8, 11, 15, 18, 21, Tom McGrath, 17; Shutterstock: dalmingo, 28, Firstear, 4-5

Artistic Credits
Shutterstock: argus, foxie, homydesign, Kompaniets Taras, Lora liu, Oleg
Golovnev, Picsfire, Rashevska Nataliia, xpixel

Printed in the United States of America in Stevens Point, Wisconsin.
052014   008092WZF14

Table of Contents

A World of Wicked Creatures

Do you know of any scary, dark caves near where you live? What about a creepy old house that nobody seems to live in? Have you ever walked by these places and felt freaked out? Maybe you heard some strange noises or thought you saw something moving in the shadows. Don't worry, it was probably just your imagination—or was it? Perhaps it was a boggart, goblin, or gremlin hiding in the dark! After all, stories about wicked creatures such as these have been around for a very long time.

Could the creatures in these old stories be real? Fortunately, no. Evil creatures like orcs and hags live only in our imaginations. Long ago people often made up stories to explain things they didn't understand. When things suddenly disappeared or were mysteriously destroyed, it was often blamed on wicked imaginary creatures. Today we know such creatures aren't real. But they continue to play a big role in many popular books, movies, TV shows, and more.

Let's imagine for a time that orcs, hobgoblins, and other wicked creatures are real and alive in the world today. If you wanted to find them, how would you look for them? Where do they live? What do they eat? Are they ever friendly, or do they always attack you on sight? Get ready for adventure as you learn more about several wicked creatures and how they'd behave if they were real.

Pixies

Size:
6 to 8 inches
(15 to 20 centimeters) tall

Habitat:
hollow trees, logs,
and similar spaces in
wooded areas

Diet:
seeds, nuts, wild berries,
mushrooms, honey

Life Cycle: Pixie families usually include five to six members. Mothers have a child about every 10 to 15 years. Pixie children grow quickly and reach adult size by age 10. However, they **mature** slowly and are not considered adults until at least age 50. Like their fairy cousins, adult pixies do not appear to age. Most pixies live for about 300 years.

Physical Features: At first glance it's easy to mistake pixies for fairies. Also known as sprites, pixies usually appear as tiny women. They have large eyes, pointed ears, and butterfly-like wings. But unlike fairies, pixies usually have black or dark brown hair. Their clothing is often made from dead leaves and grass or bits of dark cloth found while exploring.

Behavior: Pixies are not naturally wicked or evil. Yet they love to play tricks and practical jokes on people. However, their pranks often go too far and result in damage or injuries to others. For this reason, many people feel that pixies are nasty and wicked pests. Pixies are naturally curious and will travel long distances to explore the world. They also enjoy collecting small items like thimbles, toothpicks, string, and pieces of wire. Their small homes are often filled with worthless trinkets that they've stolen from others.

Fact Bright blue Cornish pixies cause a lot of mischief in *Harry Potter and the Chamber of Secrets* by J. K. Rowling. During one of Harry's classes, they break things, and pull people's hair. They even pick up one student by his ears and hang him from the ceiling!

mature -- to learn to act
in a sensible, adult way

Nixies

Size:
about 4 to 4.5 feet
(1.2 to 1.4 meters) tall

Habitat:
warm freshwater
ponds and lakes

Diet:
fish, clams, frogs,
some water plants

Life Cycle: Almost all nixies are female. It is unknown how they reproduce. But it is thought that, like frogs, nixies hatch from eggs as tadpoles. Their arms, legs, hands, and feet then develop as they grow. Nobody is certain, but many believe that nixies can live for several hundred years. Nixies live in groups called tribes. Each tribe includes 60 to 80 members.

Physical Features: It can be easy to mistake nixies for mermaids. Like mermaids, nixies live in water and have faces that resemble beautiful human women. However, instead of large tails, nixies have two strong legs with flipperlike feet that help them swim quickly. Their pale green skin is made of tiny fishlike scales. Instead of ears, nixies have **gills** that allow them to breathe underwater. Most nixies have dark green hair that resembles seaweed. They enjoy braiding shells or water lilies into their hair.

Behavior: Nixies are fiercely private and will do anything to protect their watery homes. They normally use music and magical **illusions** to draw people away from their **lairs**. However, nixies can be violent and aren't afraid of driving away intruders by force.

Nixies are usually happy to be left alone. But some nixies have a more wicked nature. They enjoy using their magical abilities to trap innocent people. These people are usually used as slaves to help guard the nixies' territory or do other work for them.

gill ⋯ a body part on the side of a fish used for breathing underwater

illusion ⋯ something that appears to be real but isn't

lair ⋯ a place where an animal lives or sleeps

Sirens

Size:
6 to 6.5 feet
(1.8 to 2 m) long

Habitat:
rocky islands
and shorelines
near the sea

Diet:
fish, oysters, sea
urchins, starfish,
octopuses; prefer
humans when possible

Life Cycle: Only a few people have ever reported seeing sirens. For this reason, little is known about these strange creatures. It's believed that sirens are all female. Some people think sirens capture human men to serve as mates, but that hasn't been proven. Nobody knows how quickly siren children grow or how long they live. Some people say that sirens can live up to 1,000 years.

Physical Features: In their true form, sirens look like monstrous mermaids. They have scaly blue or green skin. Their webbed hands are tipped with wicked claws and their mouths are filled with sharp, needlelike teeth. Sirens also have a strong tail that helps them swim quickly.

Behavior: Sirens are fierce and hungry hunters. They normally stun their prey with **sonic** blasts before eating it. However, when sirens spot unwary sailors, they use different methods. They use magical singing and illusions to cloud the sailors' minds. The sailors believe the sirens are incredibly beautiful women calling from the shore. The dazed sailors usually end up smashing their ships on nearby rocks where the sirens can easily capture them. Very few people have ever escaped from the sirens' clever traps.

sonic ⋅⋅⋅ having to do with sound waves

Hags

Size:
about 5.5 to 6 feet
(1.7 to 1.8 m) tall

Habitat:
damp caves and
broken-down shacks
in dark forests or
stinking swamps

Diet:
worms, snails, slugs,
toads, rats; prefer
eating human flesh
when possible

Life Cycle: Hags are unable to have children. They kidnap young boys and girls instead. Hags use boys for food, but they raise girls as their own. They force the girls to work as slaves until the age of 10. At this point they begin teaching the girls how to cast evil spells. By age 30 the girls are so **corrupt** and wicked they become hags themselves. Hags use powerful magic to live for hundreds or even thousands of years.

Physical Features: Hags are known for their hideous appearance. They are extremely old women with shriveled bodies, hunched backs, and filthy, stringy hair. Their noses are large and pointed, and their mouths are full of black, rotting teeth. Their skin is usually green and covered with hairy warts and open sores. Hags also have long arms and long fingers tipped with sharp black claws.

Behavior: Hags are completely evil. Their powerful evil often affects the lands where they live. When a hag moves into an area, green forests soon become dead and rotten and wetlands become stinking swamps. Hags have a strong hunger for human flesh. They often disguise themselves with magic to lure people into their lairs. Once people are inside, hags reveal their true appearance. They enjoy hearing the screams of their victims before satisfying their hunger.

corrupt ⋯ to be evil or morally decayed

★★★ FANTASY ALL-STAR

In the famous fairytale "Hansel and Gretel," an evil hag tricks the two children into entering her house and traps them. The hag plans to cook and eat them, but they outwit her. They manage to trap her inside her own oven before escaping.

Boggarts

Size:
8 to 12 inches
(20 to 30 centimeters) tall

Habitat:
closets, attics, and
other seldom used
spaces in old houses

Diet:
stale bread crusts,
sour milk, moldy cheese,
and other discarded
scraps of food

Life Cycle: It's thought that boggarts are actually brownies that have been mistreated in some way. When a normally friendly brownie becomes very angry, it can turn into a wicked boggart. Some people think that if a boggart receives a sincere apology it will return to its helpful brownie form. However, boggarts have a very nasty nature, so this theory is yet to be proven. Nobody is sure how long boggarts live.

Physical Features: Boggarts appear similar to brownies, but with more monstrous features. They are bigger and more muscular, and they often have green skin. They have beady black or red eyes, long pointed ears, and coarse whiskers. Their snarling mouths are filled with sharp teeth.

Behavior: Boggarts are wicked creatures who love causing trouble and playing pranks on people. They've been known to break or steal important items, such as people's eyeglasses or keys. Boggarts often make strange noises in attics or slam doors at night to scare people. They may also pinch people's noses, pull their ears, or cut their hair while they sleep. While boggarts never kill, they aren't afraid of hurting people and causing injuries. One of their favorite tricks is to scatter tacks on the floor next to people's beds at night. Then they wake the people up with loud noises. Boggarts delight in watching their sleepy victims hurt their feet after stumbling out of bed.

Gremlins

Size:
2 to 2.5 feet
(0.6 to 0.8 m) tall

Habitat:
deep, dark
underground caves

Diet:
worms, insects,
snails, salamanders;
prefer human-made
food whenever
possible

Life Cycle: Nobody is sure how gremlins reproduce. But these **reptilian** creatures likely hatch from eggs. It's thought that females lay up to 60 eggs each year. After hatching young gremlins are left to care for themselves and grow very quickly. They usually reach adulthood in about 30 days. Gremlins live dangerously. Most are killed accidentally within a few months of hatching. Gremlins rarely live more than 8 years.

Physical Features: Often called imps, gremlins walk on two legs like humans. They have tough, scaly skin that is usually green or brown. Their large eyes are usually green, yellow, or red. Gremlins have mouths filled with jagged teeth and long fingers tipped with sharp claws. Their huge ears are shaped like bats' wings. A few gremlins may have short horns on their heads.

Behavior: Gremlins are mean and nasty. They delight in destroying things and causing as much trouble as possible. They also enjoy playing pranks on others. Gremlins care nothing about the safety of others or even themselves. If someone is injured or killed from their misdeeds, they just enjoy the prank even more. Sunlight is deadly to gremlins and they don't like bright moonlight. They live deep underground and come to the surface to cause trouble only on the darkest of nights.

FANTASY ALL-STAR

In the hit 1980s film *Gremlins*, the main monsters begin as furry creatures called mogwais. When they eat food after midnight, they transform into dangerous gremlins. The gremlins cause a lot of damage and trouble before they're finally defeated.

reptilian ⋯ having characteristics similar to a reptile

17

Goblins

Size:
4 to 4.5 feet
(1.2 to 1.4 m) tall

Habitat:
dark mountain caves

Diet:
worms, insects, mushrooms, all types of meat; prefer gnomes when possible

Life Cycle: Goblins live in large **colonies** and reproduce quickly. Females have three to four babies each year. Young goblins grow quickly and reach adulthood within one year. Most goblins are killed at a young age during battles or fighting among themselves. A few goblins may live up to 20 years.

Physical Features: Goblins look similar to orcs and are often mistaken for them. However, goblins are generally shorter and smaller than orcs. Goblins also stand or walk in a bent over posture. They have large pointed ears and mouths full of sharp jagged teeth. Goblins have very large yellow or green eyes, which help them see in the dark. Bright light is painful for them. Goblins hate the sun and never leave their dark caves during the day.

Behavior: Goblins don't produce food or many useful tools of their own. They instead raid nearby farms or villages at night to steal what they need. However, goblins are clever at making simple weapons and traps to protect their underground homes.

Fact In several stories goblins love treasure as much as dragons do. They often steal shiny jewels or trinkets from other goblins to add to their own collections. This behavior usually leads to deadly fights between them.

colony ⋅⋅ a large group of creatures living together in the same area

Hobgoblins

Size:
5.5 to 6 feet
(1.7 to 1.8 m) tall

Habitat:
mountain caves; ruins
of castles and forts in
mountainous regions

Diet:
potatoes, rabbits, sheep,
goats, gnomes, goblins;
prefer dwarves when possible

Life Cycle: Like goblins, hobgoblins reproduce quickly.
Females give birth to one or two babies per year. Children grow
quickly and are considered adults by age 3. Hobgoblins are
naturally violent and most die or are killed in battle at a young
age. Hobgoblins usually live no more than 35 years.

Physical Features: Hobgoblins are related to goblins and
orcs, but they have some unique features. These wicked creatures
have muscular bodies covered in coarse brown or black hair. Their
eyes are usually yellow or red. Hobgoblins have mouths full of
sharp teeth and two large tusks in their lower jaws. Many
hobgoblins weave bits of bone or metal trinkets into their long
hair and beards.

Behavior: Hobgoblin **society** is based on a military lifestyle.
Children begin training to fight as soon as they can walk and
carry a weapon. Hobgoblins are intelligent and skilled at creating
complex weapons such as **crossbows**. They are also fierce and
tireless fighters. Once they enter battle they keep fighting until
they either win or are killed.

society — a group that shares the same laws,
beliefs, and customs

crossbow — a type of bow that is held and
fired with a trigger like a gun

Fact In many stories, goblins, hobgoblins, and orcs fight against dwarves for territory in the mountains. For this reason, these creatures and dwarves are natural enemies. They always attack each other on sight.

Fact Orcs have a natural hatred of elves in most stories. They hate nature, beautiful art, and other things that elves love. Being natural enemies, orcs and elves usually attack and try to kill each other any chance they get.

Orcs

Size:
4.5 to 5 feet
(1.4 to 1.5 m) tall

Habitat:
mountain caves;
deserted castles
or forts

Diet:
rats, squirrels, rabbits,
deer, goats, and other
meat; prefer elves
when possible

Life Cycle: Orc colonies always have large populations. It's believed that females are kept hidden and have up to three babies per year. Orc children likely grow very quickly and reach adulthood within two years. Some people think orcs may naturally live for hundreds of years. However, because of their violent natures, orcs rarely live beyond 50 years.

Physical Features: Orcs have a wide variety of appearances. Their skin can be black, gray, green, red-brown, or pale white in color. They may have long, greasy hair or no hair at all. Their bodies can be short and squat or lean and muscular. Nearly all orcs have ugly, deformed faces, pointed ears, and crooked mouths full of jagged teeth. Their squinty yellow eyes are sensitive to sunlight. Many orcs take pride in their nasty scars left from injuries they've received in combat.

Behavior: Orcs are cruel and violent creatures with short tempers. They often fight violently over minor disagreements. Most orcs aren't very intelligent, but they can be clever craftsmen. They often make ugly yet effective weapons and armor from wood, metal, and bone. Orcs enjoy destroying things and creating violence. They'll often burn entire villages and kill or capture every person in them. Captured people are usually forced to work as slaves and are given little food, water, or rest.

Black Orcs

Size:
6.5 to 7 feet
(2 to 2.1 m) tall

Habitat:
mountain caves
or strong forts
controlled by
evil warlords

Diet:
rats, rabbits, goats,
deer, or any other
kind of meat;
prefer humans
whenever possible

Life Cycle: Black orcs aren't born as babies. Instead, evil wizards and warlords grow them in special underground chambers. It takes about one week for black orcs to become fully grown. They are then removed from the chambers, given a sword, and immediately begin combat training. Black orcs are forced to fight until they win or are killed. It's unknown how long they may live naturally.

Physical Features: Black orcs have big, muscular bodies and large, strong hands. Their black skin is thick and tough, which is often marked by thick scars from fighting in battle. Black orcs have yellow eyes, pointed ears, and greasy black hair, although some shave their heads. Black orcs' snarling mouths are filled with sharp, jagged teeth. Some also have large fangs pointing up from their lower jaws.

Behavior: Black orcs are the biggest and strongest of all goblin-type creatures. They are violent, cruel, and have short tempers. They don't care about others and will kill anyone who dares to insult them.

Black orcs are highly skilled warriors. From their first breath they are taught how to fight. They are intelligent and often use clever battle plans to attack enemies. They also know how to build and use complex weapons such as crossbows and **catapults**. Given enough time, an army of black orcs can defeat even the strongest fortress.

catapult -- a weapon used to hurl large rocks or other objects at enemies

FANTASY ALL-STAR

The blockbuster 2001 film *The Lord of the Rings: The Fellowship of the Ring* features a huge black orc chieftain named Lurtz. He leads a raiding party to find and capture the story's heroes. Lurtz is killed by Aragorn, a heroic fighter who later becomes a king.

Troglodytes

Size:
5 to 5.5 feet
(1.5 to 1.7 m) tall

Habitat:
underground caves
or dark swamps

Diet:
fish, frogs, snakes,
birds, muskrats; prefer
humans when possible

Life Cycle:
Troglodytes lay four or five eggs once per year. The eggs hatch about eight weeks after being laid. Mothers care for their young for about six months or until they can care for themselves. Young troglodytes live difficult and violent lives. Many die or are killed at a young age. If they reach adulthood at age 30, they officially become part of the tribe. Troglodytes can live up to 130 years.

Physical Features:
Troglodytes are sometimes called lizard men. They have muscular bodies with scaly green or blue-green skin. Their lizardlike eyes are usually green or yellow and help them see well in the dark. Troglodytes have very strong jaws and mouths filled with razor-sharp teeth. They also have long, powerful tails similar to alligator tails. Male troglodytes have colorful **frills** that run from their heads down the back of their necks.

Behavior:
Troglodytes are almost always hungry for meat and treasure. Because of this, some people think they're related to dragons. However, they don't have wings or breath weapons, so this is unlikely.

Troglodytes are strong and fierce fighters. They often raid nearby settlements to steal food, weapons, treasure—and people. Captured villagers are used as slaves, food, or **sacrifices** to their gods.

frill ⋯ a flap of skin on a reptile's head or neck
sacrifice ⋯ something offered as a gift to a god

Legends Around the World

𝔓 Pixies

Pixies are found in many stories and folktales from England. In one story from Cornwall, England, a pixie named "Omfra" loses his laugh. He searches for a long time until King Arthur restores his laugh in the form of a bird. Another tale describes "Joan the Wad," who was the queen of the pixies. She carries a torch to guide people and bring them good luck.

ℌ Hags

Old folktales and stories about hags are found all over Europe. Many of them were likely meant to frighten naughty children into behaving. The most famous story, "Hansel and Gretel," comes from Germany. Children in Russia know the story of "Baba Yaga." She was an old hag who lived in a strange hut that had legs like a chicken's. In a scary story from England, "Jenny Greenteeth" is a river hag who pulls people into the water and drowns them.

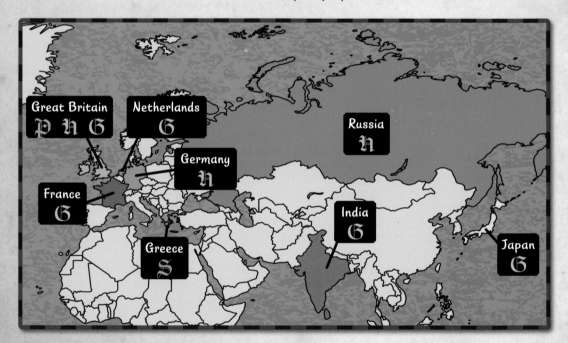

𝔖 Sirens

Sirens are one of many fantastic creatures found in ancient Greek myths. The Greek poet Homer writes about sirens in his poem the *Odyssey*. In the story the hero Odysseus and his ship's crew avoid the sirens' magical singing by plugging their ears with beeswax.

𝔊 Goblins

Tales about goblins are common in Europe. Stories like "The Benevolent Goblin," "The Goblin Pony," and "The Goblins Turned to Stone" come from England, France, and the Netherlands. But goblin stories are found in other parts of the world as well. These include "The Goblin Rat" from Japan and "Twenty-Two Goblins" from India.

Test Your Knowledge

Do you feel confident in your knowledge of goblins, hags, orcs, and other nasty creatures? Take this short quiz to test yourself. Do you have what it takes to become an expert on wicked fantasy creatures?

1 **If you're sailing at sea and you see a beautiful woman singing and waving to you from shore, it is likely to be a:**

  A. pixie.

  B. siren.

  C. nixie.

2 **How do hags reproduce?**

  A. They have a baby once every five years.

  B. They use dark magic to create a child.

  C. They kidnap young girls and teach them to become hags.

3 **The best way to deal with a boggart is to:**

  A. give a sincere apology for any offenses.

  B. expose it to sunlight.

  C. offer it money to leave you alone.

4 **Which of the following do orcs hate the most?**

  A. dwarves

  B. hobgoblins

  C. elves

5 **Which wicked creatures are the best warriors?**

  A. orcs

  B. black orcs

  C. hobgoblins

6 **Gremlins are best known for:**

  A. playing pranks on people and destroying things.

  B. creating clever weapons and traps.

  C. raiding nearby villages to steal food.

Glossary

catapult (KAT-uh-puhlt) ⤙ a weapon used to hurl large rocks or other objects at enemies

colony (KAH-luh-nee) ⤙ a large group of creatures that live together in the same area

corrupt (kuh-RUPT) ⤙ to be evil or morally decayed

crossbow (KRAWS-boh) ⤙ a type of bow that is held and fired with a trigger like a gun

frill (FRIL) ⤙ a flap of skin on a reptile's head or neck

gill (GIL) ⤙ a body part on the side of a fish used for breathing underwater

illusion (i-LOO-zhuhn) ⤙ something that appears to be real but isn't

lair (LAYR) ⤙ a place where an animal lives or sleeps

mature (muh-TOOR) ⤙ to learn to act in a sensible, adult way

reptilian (rep-TIL-ee-uhn) ⤙ having characteristics similar to a reptile

sacrifice (SAK-ruh-fisse) ⤙ something offered as a gift to a god

society (suh-SYE-uh-tee) ⤙ a group that shares the same laws, beliefs, and customs

sonic (SON-ik) ⤙ having to do with sound waves

Read More

Berk, Ari. *The Secret History of Hobgoblins.* Somerville, Mass.: Candlewick Press, 2012.

Cox, Barbara, and Scott Forbes. *Spooky Spirits and Creepy Creatures.* Creepy Chronicles. New York: Gareth Stevens, 2014.

Sparrow, Giles. *Field Guide to Fantastic Creatures.* London: Quercus Books, 2009.

Internet Sites

FactHound offers a safe, fun way to find Internet sites related to this book. All of the sites on FactHound have been researched by our staff.

Here's all you do:

Visit *www.facthound.com*

Type in this code: 9781491406892

 Check out projects, games and lots more at **www.capstonekids.com**

Index